BREEDERS' BEST

A KENNEL CLUB BOOK

Chow Chow

By Dr. Samuel Draper

BREEDERS' BEST™

A KENNEL CLUB BOOK®

CHOW CHOW

ISBN: 1-59378-935-1

Copyright © 2004

Kennel Club Books, LLC
308 Main Street, Allenhurst, NJ 07711 USA
Printed in South Korea

PHOTOS BY:
Paulette Braun, Ashbey Photography,
Isabelle Français, Kathy France
and Marilyn Magusinale

Special thanks to owners:
Elaine & Linda Albert,
George and Kathy Beliew,
Paulette Braun, Sam Draper,
Wayne and Lynda Eyster and Karen Tracy.

DRAWINGS BY:
Bandin.

Contents

Meet the Chow Chow

A magnificent animal with all of the Chinese mystique about him, the Chow Chow is quiet, refined, dignified and aloof. He is unique, smart, devoted and noble. However, with all of these wonderful traits, you should know that he can be stubborn, he can be indifferent and he will take over the household if given half a chance. Are you thinking of adding a Chow Chow to your household? If so, read on about this breed and see if this is the dog

With his abundant mane and regal scowl, the Rough Chow Chow is no cowardly lion, but rather a dignified dog with a unique personality to be understood by a special kind of owner.

for you and your family.

The Chow Chow is one of the most ancient of canine breeds in the world. He was known as far back as the 11th century BC, when it was thought that marauding invaders from the Arctic brought their dogs south with them. These dogs were described as warrior dogs who were strong and extremely tough, migrating from the Arctic through Siberia and Mongolia, and eventually into China. The descendants of these dogs were probably those known as the Northern canines, which would include the Norwegian Elkhound, the Samoyed, the Keeshond and even the tiny Pomeranian, all of which have certain similarities.

The Smooth Chow has a shorter, yet still very dense, coat and the same regal bearing as his Rough counterpart.

The Chow Chow was originally used as a hunting dog and the story is told that, in the 7th century AD, one of the emperors kept 2,500 Chows to accompany his 10,000 hunters in the field. In addition to their hunting

The Chow Chow and Pug are compatriots, sharing China as their country of ancestry.

abilities, these dogs were also used for guarding livestock and, on occasion, for herding large herds of cattle. And it must be mentioned, as unpleasant as it may be to us, that the Chow was also used as a source of food.

The Chow's look has always been different from that of other breeds, as the Chow has a large head, small eyes and a profuse ruff around his neck, and is very straight in the legs. No wonder the breed was

The Chow Chow is distinct in his physical traits, perhaps the most interesting being his bluish-black tongue.

called "Lion Dog." His most outstanding physical characteristic, shared by no other breed, is his blue-black tongue.

The Chow first appeared in England as early as the 1780s; however, his popularity did not rise until the 1860s, when the Earl of Lonsdale became a strong supporter of the breed. Making frequent trips to the Far East, the earl was presented with a Chow Chow, which he brought back to England and presented to his relatives, the Marquis and Marchioness of Huntley. The breed immediately caught the fancy of the royals, and they requested that more Chows be brought back to England when future trips were taken to the East. The Marchioness became well known as the first important and influential breeder of Chows in the UK. Peridot II, out of the Marchioness's Peridot, won a prestigious all-breed Best in Show in 1895 at the Ladies Kennel Club Championship show, becoming the first big Chow winner in England.

Up until 1893, the Chow was entered in the "foreign dog" class at shows but, after that time, he had his own classification. By 1896, the breed was eligible to win Challenge Certificates (necessary for a UK championship). The first Chow was registered in the UK in 1894. On July 1, 1895, the breeders of note met to form the Chow Chow Club. The first notable Chow winner from this era was Ch. Blue Blood, the first English-bred Chow to gain his championship.

The Chow appeared on the scene in the US as early as 1890, when a dog was listed in the Westminster Kennel Club catalog as a "Chinese Chow Chow dog." The first American champion was Chinese Chum, an English import, who also won the breed at Westminster in 1906 and later sired some exceptional progeny.

Many breeders played an important role in the development of the breed in America. However, it should be

Is there any question why this breed has been referred to as the "Lion Dog"?

mentioned that Mrs. E. K. Lincoln's Greenacre Chows were certainly at the forefront of the winning Chows in the early 1900s, with a number of Bests of Breed at the Westminster Kennel Club. Her kennel, active for over 20 years, produced about 50 champions.

Early breeders and kennels in the 1920s who made an impact upon the breed with their outstanding dogs were the

Clairedale Chows of Claire Knapp Penny, Flora Bonney and Kathleen Staples (and the excellent dogs that they purchased from Claire Penny) and the Yang Fu kennels in Milwaukee, Wisconsin.

In the 1920s, the Chow took a surge in popularity, helped by the fact that President Calvin Coolidge kept his pet Chow at the White House and the public had a chance to see and become familiar with the breed. During this period, many poorly bred Chows with poor dispositions appeared on the scene, and the breed fell from favor with the American public. Those dedicated to the breed worked to breed better dogs with outstanding dispositions and, through time, succeeded to such an extent that the Chow once again became popular with the public.

In the 1950s, Ch. Ghat de la Moulaine was imported from France by Clif and Vivian Shyrock of Hawaiian Gardens, California. This dog became a major force within the breed, being not only a great show dog but also a great producer whose offspring, in turn, became great both in the ring and through their offspring.

The author, a judge from the East Coast, had been breeding Chows since the late 1960s. With Mr. and Mrs. Robert Hetherington, he purchased Ch. Eastward Liontamer of Elster from Merilyn Morgan in California and brought him east. This dog became a great Chow, with 10 all-breed Bests in Show, 52 Non-Sporting Groups and over 300 Best of Breed wins. Joel

In today's show rings, the Chow Chow glistens with confidence and an alluring aloofness that is all its own.

Marston, of Starcrest Kennels from the West Coast, was also breeding and showing beautiful well-bred dogs during the same time period. Both the author and Mr. Marston did much for the Chow breed, producing fine animals with excellent dispositions. Chows were well-known throughout the country. A judge who greatly admired the breed said that the Chows were good "from border to border, coast to coast. Chows of quality and merit have made their contribution to this distinguished breed."

The breed continues to be on good footing throughout the world, with a very devout group of fanciers, breeders and exhibitors behind it. It places in the the top half of American Kennel Club (AKC) breeds in popularity and ranks comparably in Great Britain. There also are numerous Chow breeders throughout Canada who are producing fine dogs, many that have been exported to other countries.

MEET THE CHOW CHOW

Overview

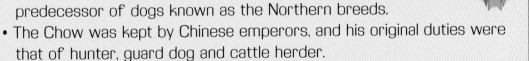
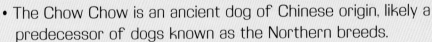

- The Chow Chow is an ancient dog of Chinese origin, likely a predecessor of dogs known as the Northern breeds.
- The Chow was kept by Chinese emperors, and his original duties were that of hunter, guard dog and cattle herder.
- The Chow's large, distinct head and scowling expression earned him the moniker "Lion Dog."
- The first Chow in England was brought there from China; quite some time later, the first dog on the US scene was an English import.
- Breeders had to work to stabilize the breed's temperament. Fine Chow Chows are now bred across the US, Canada and the UK, and most other countries around the world.

CHAPTER 2

Description of the Chow Chow

E very breed of dog registered with the American Kennel Club has an official written standard, describing what the ideal member of the breed should look and act like. The Chow Chow is in the AKC's Non-Sporting Group. In general, the dogs in this group are basically companion dogs today, though they were once used for a variety of tasks.

Other dogs in this group include the Bulldog, French Bulldog, Dalmatian, Boston Terrier and Standard and Miniature Poodles.

The Chow Chow is a medium-sized, squarely built dog with heavy bone and a sturdy appearance.

The Chow, even though he is now thought of as a rather exotic companion dog, was once an all-purpose dog used for hunting, herding, pulling and guarding the household. He is a medium-sized dog with heavy bone, squarely built. He is compact and short in length, and he has a large head. He is a very handsome and proud animal. The Chow can be anywhere between 17 and 20 inches in height at the shoulder, with the females being slightly smaller than the males.

The Chow is seen in various solid colors: red, black, blue, cinnamon and cream, but all should have the characteristic blue tongue.

For the Chow, the head is a very important feature. It should be large and proudly carried but should not be so large as to make the dog look out of balance. His expression, as described in the standard, is "essentially scowling, dignified, lordly, discerning, sober and snobbish, one of independence." The correct eye shape and placement and the brow all contribute to the expression.

The Chow's dignified leonine expression is aptly described as "scowling."

Occiput: Upper back part of skull; apex.

Skull: Cranium.

Stop: Indentation between the eyes at point of nasal bones and skull.

Muzzle: Foreface or region of head in front of eyes.

Flews: Hanging part of upper lip.

Lips: Fleshy portion of upper and lower jaws.

Withers: Highest part of the back, at the base of neck above the shoulders.

Shoulder: Upper point of forequarters; the region of the two shoulder blades.

Forechest: Sternum.

Chest: Thoracic cavity (enclosed by ribs).

Forequarters: Front assembly from shoulder to feet.

Upper arm: Region between shoulder blade and forearm.

Elbow: Region where upper arm and forearm meet.

Forearm: Region between elbow and wrist.

Carpus: Wrist.

Dewclaw: Extra digit on inside of leg; fifth toe.

Brisket: Lower chest.

Back: Dorsal surface, extending from the withers.

Topline: Outline from withers to tailset.

Loin: Lumbar region between ribs and pelvis.

Body: Region between fore- and hindquarters.

Stern: Tail.

Croup: Pelvic region; rump.

Hip: Joint of pelvis and upper thigh bone.

Hindquarters: Rear assembly from pelvis to feet.

Upper thigh: Region from hip joint to stifle.

Stifle: Knee.

Lower thigh: Hindquarter region from stifle to hock; second thigh.

Hock: Tarsus or heel.

Pastern: Region between heel (or wrist) and toes.

Flank: Region between last rib and hip.

Abdomen: Surface beneath the chest and hindquarters; belly.

Digit: Toe.

The Chow's ears are small, triangular in shape and placed wide apart. In no way is the ear to drop. His skull and muzzle both are broad and give the appearance of being square. Of course, the most unique physical trait of the Chow is the color of his tongue. A blue-black tongue is called for, the darker the better.

He has a strong neck and a short, compact body. His chest is broad and deep and he has strong shoulders, which are well muscled. This is one of the few breeds in which the rear legs are straight, with little angulation, which produces a distinct-looking gait. His gait "must be sound, straight moving, agile, brief, quick and powerful, never lumbering. It is from the side that the unique

Broad in skull and muzzle, the Chow possesses small triangular ears and an unmistakable scowling expression.

stilted action is most easily assessed."

The breed is seen in two types of coats, the rough and the smooth, with both having an undercoat. There is no trimming done to the coat, but the feet should be neatened up with scissors; trimming of the whiskers is optional. His colors are solid or solid with lighter shadings, and the accepted colors are red (light golden to deep mahogany), black, blue, cinnamon (light fawn to deep cinnamon) and cream. There is no preference among the colors. The breed standard for the Rough Chow and the Smooth Chow is the same, with the only difference being the type of coat.

The temperament of the Chow is very important. He will be reserved and careful with strangers, but "keen intelligence, an independent spirit and innate dignity gives him an aura of aloofness." The standard stresses that "displays of aggression or timidity are unacceptable.

DESCRIPTION OF THE CHOW CHOW

Overview

- The head is perhaps the Chow Chow's most important feature. It is large and proud, with the trademark scowl and, of course, the breed's unique blue-black tongue.
- The Chow is medium in size, square in build and heavy in bone.
- The Chow's gait is a quick stilted action, due to his straight hind legs.
- The coat is seen in two varieties: rough, which is more common, and smooth. The breed is accepted in a range of solid colors.
- The Chow Chow gives off an air of aloofness. While he is reserved, dignified and intelligent, he should be neither shy nor aggressive.

Are You a Chow Chow Person?

B efore purchasing a Chow Chow, you must give some thought to the personality and characteristics of this breed to determine if this is the dog for you. This is not a breed for the laid-back owner who will not give the dog the training and attention that he deserves. In addition, this may not always be a good choice for the first-time puppy owner. This is a dog for the individual who has studied up on the breed, understands its characteristics and is willing to train the dog, to accept his disposition and to give him

Are you ready for this lion of a dog and all the care, training and grooming that comes along with him?

the time that he will need for socialization.

You should answer the following
questions before purchasing a Chow:

1. Do you have the time to give to a
   dog? He will need care, companionship, training and grooming.
   This is almost like having a child,
   except that the dog remains
   childlike in that he will always
   require your care.

Paulette and Chen have a wonderful
dog/owner bond. It takes a special
person to build such a close relationship with a Chow.

2. Do you have a fenced yard for your
   Chow? This is not a dog that you
   can leave tied out on the porch. He
   must have a secure area in which
   to run and exercise.

3. Have you owned a dog previously
   and did that dog live a long and
   happy life with your family?

4. Are you willing to have a dog who
   will be independent, who will have
   a mind of his own in addition to a
   stubborn streak? A dog who may
   sometimes be indifferent to what
   you are doing? Are you patient?

The Chow Chow likes to have "only
child" status in the family and may
not warm up right away to the kids,
making early socialization from
puppyhood ever so essential to
ensure that he becomes a happy
member of the family.

5. Do you have the time, and are you willing, to spend a few hours every week grooming your dog?
6. Are there other pets in your household?

Let's take each question one at a time.

1. Having time for a dog does not mean that you cannot work and own a dog. Your pet will need quality time, though, just like a child needs it. He must be fed two times a day and exercised several times a day. He needs to be cared for, and he may even like to go for rides in the car with

Starrlett gets the star treatment with her own cozy dog bed in her owner's bedroom.

you. You must work with him to have an obedient dog who has good manners. It is very important to socialize your Chow, and this will take time and patience. Your dog should have at least two good outings a day, and that means a walk or a good romp in the morning and the evening. You need to make time to take your Chow out and about; this means taking him shopping, visiting the park, walking down Main Street, etc. He needs to see people and to be seen! On that note, however, never let him out loose to run the neighborhood.

2. If you have a fenced property, you should have enough space to throw a ball and for your dog to run with it...if he chooses! Remember, it is your responsibility to keep the yard clean of feces, for the sake of cleanliness for the

dog and your family members. When walking your dog, it is essential to carry a plastic bag or two to pick up droppings. These will be unlike that of dogs of other breeds. You must understand the personality and disposition of the Chow in order to do him

The Chow Chow is not the best choice for a multiple-pet household, but that doesn't mean he can't learn to befriend other canines.

can be easily dropped in a handy trash receptacle on your way home. In many towns, this is the law.

3. Having owned a dog previously will give you a good idea of what a dog expects from you and what you must do for your dog. But do bear in mind that what the Chow expects from you justice and to have a good pet for the family. The Chow is smart and needs an owner who is equally as smart as, or smarter than, he is!

4. Do not expect the Chow to lie on your lap for the evening. He may like to spend time in his own way, probably lying near you,

but he likely won't fawn over you as some breeds will. He does thrive on human companionship— but on occasion he may become so happy with his family that he is not well socialized with other individuals. You must guard against this with the Chow and not let him become an anti-social animal. Also, do

Remember the Chow Chow's origins and history to help you relate to the breed's temperament.

not purchase the Chow if you are looking for a breed to roughhouse with your children. The Chow will not tolerate that kind of behavior.

5. Do you have the time and interest to groom a Chow? The Chow comes in two coats, the rough coat, which is the Chow that you usually see, and the smooth coat. The rough coat, with its big neck ruff and heavy, dense undercoat, will require grooming twice a week, possibly more when the dog sheds his coat. The smooth-coated Chow will also require grooming, but there will be much less coat to groom. You will not have a happy pet, or be a happy Chow owner, if you do not keep the coat brushed, mat-free and clean.

6. The Chow thrives best as an "only child." Chows often do not get along well with other pets, and you may have a stressful situation if you bring a Chow into a family that already has one or two, or more, pets. You do not want any difficult situations to arise that you cannot control, so it is best to talk this over with the

breeder of your Chow puppy before you bring him home. Don't worry—the Chow is more than enough dog for anyone.

For more information on the Chow Chow, you can find an excellent source on the Internet with the Chow Chow Club Inc.'s website: www.chowclub.org. This website is a trusted source of information from experienced breed people in addition to giving you listings of local Chow Chow clubs and breeders.

Chows on patrol! One of breed's original duties was that of guard dog, so don't be surprised if your Chow takes it upon himself to keep watch over the home and yard.

ARE YOU A CHOW CHOW PERSON?

Overview

- The Chow is not suitable for owners who do not understand the breed's unique temperament.
- Think about whether you are ready for dog ownership in general and, more specifically, Chow ownership.
- The Chow is loyal to his owners, but he is not a dog that will shower his family with affection.
- The Chow prefers life as an "only child," but, nonetheless, he must be well socialized with people, other animals and different experiences to become a well-adjusted dog that is stable in temperament.

Selecting a Breeder

When you buy your Chow, you will want to buy a healthy puppy from a responsible breeder. A responsible breeder is someone who has given considerable thought before breeding his bitch. He considers health problems in the breed, has room in his home or kennel for a litter of puppies and has the time to give to a litter. He does not breed to the dog down the block because it is easy and because he wants to show his children the miracle of birth.

A responsible breeder is someone

A good breeder knows the Chow and understands the breed's temperament. She is attentive to each puppy, taking time to handle them and acclimate them to humans.

who is dedicated to the breed and to breeding out any faults and hereditary problems, and whose overall interest is in improving the breed. He will study pedigrees and see what the leading stud dogs are producing. To find the right stud dog for his bitch, he may fly his bitch across the country to breed to a particular stud dog, or he may drive the bitch to the dog, who may be located a considerable distance away. He may have only one or two litters per year, which means that there may not be a puppy ready for you when you first call. Remember that you are purchasing a new family member and that usually the wait will be well worthwhile.

Only consider buying a puppy from a breeder who has the litter's dam available for you to see. Puppies must stay with their mother for at least the first eight weeks, during which time you'll be making your visits.

Check out the Chow Chow Club's website at www.chowclub.org for a listing of regional breed clubs in the US. You should be able to find one in your state or at least in your region, as there are affiliate clubs across the country. The regional club should be able

A Chow Chow litter is a mixture of teddy-bear cuteness and lionlike confidence.

to refer you to a responsible breeder in your area and should be able to answer any questions that you may have.

The responsible Chow breeder will probably be someone who has been breeding Chows for some years and someone who is known on the national level. He will be a member of the local Chow Chow club, if there is one, and will also belong to the national parent club and possibly an all-breed kennel club.

The responsible breeder will show you his kennel, if he has a kennel, or invite you into his home to see the puppies. The areas will be clean and smell good. The breeder will show you the dam of the litter that you are looking at and she will be clean, smell good and be groomed. The puppies will also be clean, with trimmed toenails and clean faces. He may only show you a few puppies, as he may not show you the puppies that are already sold or that he is going to keep.

The breeder will

Does this photograph reflect the achievements represented in your Chow Chow pup's family tree? It should!

also have questions for you. Have you had a dog before? How many have you had and have you ever owned a Chow? Did your dogs live long lives? Do you have a fenced yard? How many children do you have and what are their ages? Are you willing to spend the time to teach your children how to treat the new family member? Have you ever done any dog training and are you willing to go to obedience classes with your dog? Are there any other pets in your household? Do not be offended by these questions. The breeder has put a lot of effort and money into his litter and his first priority is to place the pups in caring and appropriate households where they will be wanted, loved and cared for.

SELECTING A BREEDER

Overview

- The Chow is a breed unique in physical traits and temperament. You must find an experienced, responsible breeder, dedicated to producing healthy, typical and sound examples of the breed.
- The Chow Chow Club of America is a trusted source of breed information and referrals to breeders across the country.
- When visiting a breeder, you will observe the puppies and the premises, as well as ask many questions about his knowledge of the breed, his breeding program, the dogs' backgrounds and the puppies' care.
- Likewise, the breeder will interview you, as a good breeder must be assured that each and every puppy is placed with a knowledgeable, caring owner who is properly prepared for Chow ownership.

Finding the Right Puppy

Sit up and take notice of the features of a well-bred Chow Chow. This nine-week-old Rough puppy easily qualifies as "pick of the litter."

Before seeing the breeder and his pups, you should give some consideration as to whether you prefer to have a male or a female for a pet. Some individuals consider males easier to obedience-train but the more aggressive of the two sexes. Males may be more difficult to house-train. Others prefer the softer disposition of a female. There are several points that should be considered in making your decision. In the Chow, the females will be a little smaller overall than the males and an inch or two shorter in height. If you have a show- or breeding-quality pup that you do not plan to neuter or spay (most breeders will require you to neuter/spay your pet-only dog or bitch), the female will come into season approximately every six months. This can be a difficult time for up to three weeks, as it is fairly messy, especially with the rough-coated Chow, and hard on the house. It will also attract any loose males in the neighborhood, who will sit on your doorstep like lovelorn swains. Males who are not neutered can be more aggressive and will have more of a tendency to lift their legs and mount your leg! If you are not sure which sex you want, discuss it with the breeder; he will be able to give you some direction.

Check your prospect's teeth and mouth to ensure that a correct bite is developing and that he possesses the blue tongue characteristic of the breed.

When looking over the pups in the breeder's litter, do not pick the puppy that hangs back timidly. Also think twice before picking the extra-active, most outgoing of the litter. Hyper

Breeders may have more than one litter on the premises. This handsome duo is an eight-month-old male and a seven-week-old female.

puppies can turn into hyper adults and will require more patience and time in training. Look for the middle-of-the-road puppy, the one that is interested, comes up to you, listens when you speak and looks very alert. Never, but *never*, pick the pup that will not approach you. Never pick a puppy because you "feel sorry" for him. Don't forget that you are adding a new member to your family and you want one that is bright, healthy and, of course, fun!

Since the Chow comes in two coat types, you should decide which coat type you prefer. Although the Rough Chow is by far the more popular, the Smooth Chow offers all of the same qualities in an easier-to-care-for coat. The smooth coat is plush and thick, just not as long as the rough coat. Plus, the smooth coat doesn't have the heavy neck ruff. If you are planning to show the puppy, you will probably opt for a Rough

Chow, as winning with a Smooth Chow is much more difficult. The smooth coat doesn't hide any structural flaws, so when a Smooth Chow wins in the show ring, you know that the dog is truly outstanding.

Don't forget the cost factor when picking a medium-sized breed. It is going to be more expensive to feed a breed like the Chow than one like the Pekingese. In addition, the clean-up for medium breeds is more extensive than for small breeds. You will need a higher fence and a larger yard for the Chow than if you have a toy breed, where you can get away with an exercise pen or a shorter fence. In addition, the crate for a larger breed can run into a considerable amount of money, even if you buy the cheapest crate available. Small dog crates are, of course, small and less expensive. Once you have a dog, you realize that these are all factors that will take a part in your decision. But, if you haven't owned a dog before, you are not aware of some of these "unseen" expenses.

You are now ready to select your puppy. You have decided that you are a Chow person and that you can live with this very courageous, smart, rather regal and independent dog. You have done your homework and have located a responsible breeder who has a litter available.

Aside from buying a puppy, there is another option for Chow ownership. That is to adopt a "rescue" Chow. This will be a Chow who, for a wide variety of reasons, is looking for a new home. This will usually be a dog over one year of age and very often trained and housebroken. The breed rescue organization will bathe and groom the dog in addition to having a veterinarian's health certificate attesting to the good health of the dog. Usually these dogs

make marvelous pets, as they are grateful for a second chance at a loving home. Not only does the national club have an active rescue organization, but the local clubs will

also have groups of individuals working in this capacity. Rescue committees consist of very dedicated individuals who care deeply about the breed and give countless hours of their time, in addition to money, to assure that each dog will have an equal chance in life.

With the Chow, do investigate the background of the dog as much as possible, as you do not want to be taking

Raising a litter is a lot of work for a Chow mother. When you go for a visit, don't be surprised if the dam looks a little tired or out of condition due to whelping, nursing and caring for the pups; nonetheless, she should be healthy and sound.

home the problems that someone else may have instilled in this particular dog. By going through the national Chow Chow club's rescue organization, you should be assured of getting a dog with which you will be able to live.

One other option is that a

will be trained and easy to live with.

Now back to discussing puppy selection. You arrive at the appointed time and the breeder has the puppies ready for you to look at. They should be a happy bunch, clean and groomed. Their

The whole family should visit the litter. With a naturally aloof breed like the Chow Chow, it's beneficial that the pup meets all members of his new human pack early on so that he can start "warming up" to each of them.

breeder may have an older dog that he wants to place in a good home. For some breeders, once they have put a championship on a dog, they would like to move this animal into a home where he will receive the optimum of attention. Do give this some thought, as often an older dog

noses will be wet, their coats will have a glow or sheen and they will have a nice covering of flesh over their ribs. You will be ready to pick up one of these rascals and cuddle him in your arms.

For a Chow pet, there is nothing more important than temperament. The sire and dam of the litter should be personable and interested in meeting you. Breeders should only breed Chows that are friendly (as well as healthy and sound). If the dam of the litter backs away from you or keeps her distance, you can be fairly certain that her pups will have the same standoffish (unfriendly) personality. Puppies like this will be harder to socialize and live with.

You should ask the breeder if the sire and dam of the litter have had their temperaments tested. Temperament tests are offered by the American Temperament Test Society (ATTS), and responsible breeders will be familiar with this organization and will have had their animals tested. The breeder will show you the parents' score sheet and you can easily determine if these are the dogs with the personalities you are looking for. In addition, this is an excellent indication that this is a responsible breeder.

Temperament testing by the ATTS is done on dogs that are at least 18 months of age; therefore, puppies are not tested, but the sire and dam of a litter can be tested. The test is like a simulated walk through a park or a neighborhood where everyday

A puppy's first human contact is with the breeder. She handles them and gives them attention and affection to foster their future relationships with people.

situations are encountered. Neutral, friendly and threatening situations are encountered to see what the dog's reactions are to the various stimuli. Problems that are looked for are unprovoked aggression, panic without recovery and strong avoidance. Also watched is behavior toward strangers, reaction to auditory, visual and tactile stimuli and self-protective and aggressive behavior. The dog is on a loose lead for the test, which takes about ten minutes to complete. As of December 2002, the ATTS had tested only 83 Chows for temperament of which 57 passed, a 68.7% passing rate.

Some breeders will have the temperaments of their puppies tested in other ways, by either a professional, their veterinarian or another dog breeder. This will uncover the high-energy pup and the pup that is slower to respond. It will find the pup with the independent spirit and the one that will want to follow the pack. If the litter has been tested, the breeder will suggest which pup he thinks will be best for your family. If the litter has not been tested, you can do a few simple tests while you are sitting on the floor playing with the pups.

Pat your leg or snap your finger and see which pup comes up to you first. Clap your hands and see if any of the litter shies away from you. See how they play with one another. Watch for the one that has the personality that appeals to you most, as this will probably be the puppy that you will take home. Look for the puppy that appears to be "in the middle," not overly rambunctious, overly aggressive or

With a pup of any breed, you can't judge a book by its cover! All puppies look as sweet as can be, but it's a big responsibility to mold the youngster's personality into that of a well-behaved dog with whom you will enjoy sharing your life, home and heart.

submissive. You want the joyful pup, not the wild one. Spend some time selecting your puppy and, if you are hesitant, tell the breeder that you would like to go home and think it over. This is a major decision, as you are adding a family member who may be with you for 10 to 15 years. Be sure that you get the puppy that you will all be happy with.

Once you've made your choice, you are now ready for the next step: you are now on your way to bringing your new puppy into your household.

What color will you choose? It's solely a matter of personal preference. None of the recognized solid colors is given precedence over another. This is an attractive cream-colored pup.

FINDING THE RIGHT PUPPY

Overview

- Male or female? Rough or smooth coat? Do you have a color preference? Do you intend to show your Chow Chow? These are all things to think about that will guide you to the perfect puppy.
- Good temperament is a must, so you must choose carefully. It is helpful if the parents or the litter have been temperament-tested, but simple tests that you can do, along with the breeder's knowledge, will help you find a friendly, personable pup.
- Of course, all pups must be physically sound, with sturdy bodies and in good health.
- If you want to own a Chow but are not quite ready for a puppy, consider adopting an adult from the breed club's rescue scheme.

Welcoming the Chow Chow

One note about the Chow puppy: It is hard to find a cuter puppy than this breed, as he is virtually a living teddy bear! However, in spite of this cuteness, it is essential that you train and socialize your young Chow correctly.

Once you have selected your puppy and he has reached the appropriate age, you will be ready to bring your new family member home. Before welcoming your pup, however, you should buy all of the puppy necessities. These include food and water pans, a soft bristle

"What is this thing?" Your Chow puppy may never have seen a crate before you introduce him to his, so give him some time to "sniff out" the situation and become comfortable with his new doggie den.

brush and a leash and collar. You should also purchase a crate for your puppy to not only sleep in but also to spend time in when he is alone. In very short order, your puppy will learn that the crate is his second home and he will feel safe and secure when he is there. Left uncrated and alone, a pup will quickly become bored and begin to chew on the furniture, the corners of woodwork, etc. Keeping him in a confined area when you cannot supervise can eliminate these problems. Be sure to add several towels or a washable blanket to the crate so that he will be comfortable.

The two types of crates most commonly used for transporting pets are the fabric mesh on the left and the plastic airline-type on the right.

If you are driving some distance to pick up your pet, take along a towel or two, a water bowl and the leash and collar. Also take along some plastic baggies to pick up droppings and a roll of paper towels in case there are any potty accidents or carsickness.

This ten-week-old male puppy certainly will make a perfect new family member, provided you're ready for the responsibility.

Before bringing your puppy into the house, you should be aware that a small puppy can be like a toddler and that there are dangers in the household that must be eliminated. Electrical wires should be raised off the floor and hidden from view,

The wire crate is the best type of crate for use in the home, and the crate you purchase for your puppy should be large enough to comfortably house an adult Chow, whether standing, sitting or lying down.

as they are very tempting as chewable objects. Swimming pools, koi ponds and even bird baths can be very dangerous, so make certain that your puppy can't get into, or fall into, one of these miniature bodies of water. Some barricades will be necessary to prevent

Your puppy will be ready to "Chow" down, so have suitable food and water bowls and a supply of puppy food ready for his arrival home.

accidents. Not all dogs can swim, and those with short legs and heavy bodies, like the Chow, cannot climb out of the water. Watch your deck railings and make sure that your puppy cannot slip through the openings and fall.

If you have young children in the house, you must see that they understand that the small puppy is a living being and must be treated gently. They cannot ride on him, pull his ears, pick him up roughly or drop him. This is your responsibility! A child taught about animals at an early age can become a lifelong compassionate animal lover and

owner. Use your common sense in all things with your pup. Consider where a

young child can get into trouble, and your puppy will be right behind him!

When puppy comes into the house for the first time (after he has relieved himself outside), let him look at his new home and surroundings, then give him a light meal and a pan of water. When he is tired, take him outside for a potty trip again and then tuck him into his crate, either to take a nap or, hopefully, to sleep through the night.

The first day or two for your puppy should be fairly quiet. He will then have time to get used to his new home, surroundings and family members. The first night, he may cry a bit, but if you put a teddy bear or a soft woolly sweater in his crate, it will give him some warmth and security. A nearby ticking clock or a radio playing soft music can also be helpful.

Remember, your pup has been uprooted from his siblings, his mother and his familiar breeder, and he will need a day or two to get used to his new family. If he should cry this first night, let him be and he will eventually quiet down and

It takes a well-trained dog to just pose with slippers and not eat them! Providing chew toys and encouraging proper chewing behavior from puppyhood result in an adult dog who knows where his teeth are—and are not—allowed.

Your Chow Chow puppy needs to feel at home indoors and out. Be sure that your yard is securely fenced and that all potential dangers are removed from the environment.

sleep. By the third night, he should be well settled in. Have patience and, within a week or less, it will seem to you, your family and your puppy that you have all been together for years.

Another area of concern will be feeding your puppy and how best to do so. Nutrition for your puppy is actually very easy. Dog-food companies hire many scientists and spend millions of dollars on research to determine what will be a healthy diet for your dog. Your breeder should have been feeding a premium puppy food, and you should continue on with the same brand. As the dog matures, you will change over to the adult formula of the same dog-food brand. Do not add vitamins or anything else unless your veterinarian suggests that you do so. Do not think that, by cooking up a special diet, you will

A hungry litter around the feeding bowl. Your puppy will soon learn that he doesn't need to compete to get his share once he's in your home.

turn out a product that will be more nutritional than what the dog-food companies are providing.

Your young puppy will probably be fed three times check your dog-food bag for the amount, per pound of weight, that you should be feeding your dog daily. To the dry kibble, you can add water to moisten and

a day and perhaps as many as four times a day. As he matures, you will cut his meals to two times a day, in the morning and in the evening. By the time he reaches eight months of age, you will be changing over to the adult dog food. You can possibly a tablespoon or so of a canned dog food for flavor.

Use your dog treats wisely; don't overdo it. Give him a dog biscuit at bedtime and avoid table treats altogether. Aside from being fattening and perhaps

Your breeder will start you on your way to feeding your pup correctly by sending home a diet sheet with feeding instructions and perhaps even a few days' supply of the good-quality food that the pup has been eating up to this point.

upsetting to a dog's digestive system, some "people foods," including chocolate, onions, some kinds of nuts, grapes and raisins, are toxic to dogs. Keep a good covering of flesh over the ribs but do not let your dog become a fat boy! However, the more active the dog, the more calories he will need. And always have fresh drinking water available. This may include a bowl of water in the kitchen and another outside in the yard

Meals should be offered at the same times each day, in the same place. Pick a corner of a room, like the kitchen, to be your Chow Chow's "dinner table."

for time spent outdoors.

You are now off to an excellent start with your puppy. As the days go by, you will quickly find more items that you will need, including several tough chew toys and a retractable leash for walks in the park once he is walking politely on-lead. You will need more grooming supplies and a good pooper scooper for the yard. These items can be acquired as needed from your local pet-supply shop.

"I'm ready! Let's go!" Your puppy will let you know when he's ready to play and when he's ready to nap, as frequent rest periods are just as essential as activity for growing pups. There are no mixed signals here!

WELCOMING THE CHOW CHOW

Overview

- Welcome your "teddy bear" pup into your home by having all of the necessities on hand before his arrival.
- Even more important is puppy-proofing. All areas of the home, indoors and out, must be safe for a curious puppy, with all potential hazards eliminated from areas to which the pup will have access.
- Teach any children in the family how to treat a puppy properly.
- Allow your pup time to settle in, realizing that the move to your home is a big change in his life.
- Take the breeder's advice about how to feed your pup the best diet and how to make dietary changes as he grows up.

Socializing the Chow Chow Puppy

The Chow Chow does not enjoy the reputation of being the most friendly dog on the planet. Indeed, he is not by nature the most gregarious and outgoing dog. Breeders, however, must emphasize the importance of social-izing the Chow so that he is friendly, reliable and completely open to meeting strangers. The author, founder of Liontamer Chows, has gone out on a limb to stress how important socialization is

Well-socialized Chows are used successfully as therapy dogs in places like hospitals and nursing homes.

in Chow Chows. Chow puppies require extra effort to encourage them to be friendly and amenable to handling. In essence, owners must make every attempt to get their Chow puppies to "come out of their shells." Breeders believe that a stud dog, or show dog, is without merit unless he can be handled. Only reliably friendly Chows should be bred, so your puppy certainly should have come from gregarious parents.

Part of socialization is accustoming your Chow to riding in the car. How else are you going to get him out and about to see the sights...or at least to see the vet!

It is very difficult to socialize an adult Chow who has not been handled and loved as a puppy. This makes rescuing such an unsocialized Chow a very daunting prospect. Unfortunately, bad-tempered adult Chows have given the breed a bad reputation, to the point that many insurance companies list the Chow Chow on their lists of dangerous breeds.

Socializing your puppy is very important if you want a dog that fits

The only thing dangerous about a well-bred, well-socialized Chow Chow is the danger of falling hopelessly in love. Who wouldn't this puppy "sleigh"?

into your home and a dog that is a good companion, enjoyed by everyone. Socializing a puppy is similar to when you bring home a new baby. Hold and pet your puppy so that he knows that he is wanted and loved. Do not play with him constantly, as he is very young and needs time to rest up and sleep. Keep him to a schedule as much as you can, as he will become schedule-oriented very quickly. If he knows that you rise at 7:00 every morning, and shortly after you will take him out, he will wait for you to let him out and will not relieve himself in his crate.

Habits, and that includes good and bad habits, that are learned at an early age become lifelong habits, so it is best to start out on the right foot (or paw). Don't let him chew on the leg of the old kitchen table and think that it's cute, because before long he will have chewed on the leg of your expensive dining-room table. Set limits and make sure that the pup sticks to them.

Keep him confined to a specific area, such as the kitchen and den, until he is trained and fairly mature. Use baby gates to block doorways and he will quickly learn that he is welcome in certain areas of the house and not welcome in other areas. And, of course, put him into his crate when you leave home, as he will be comfortable in his "house" and will sleep until you return.

Here are some basic principles for socializing the Chow Chow. Lift up your puppy and give him face-to-face loving. Tell him that he's a handsome boy (or a darling girl). The puppy may squirm or squeal, but in time he will accept your handling. Socialization is the process by which the Chow gets to like being handled. Pick him up as often as you can! If you're home with the puppy all day, make this your ritual every time you enter the room. When a friend comes to visit, or your son or daughter comes home from school, pass the puppy to him or her. Let other people handle the games with you and your young friends.

Because Chows can be somewhat independent and indifferent to people, early socialization is very important with this breed. When a stranger to your dog comes

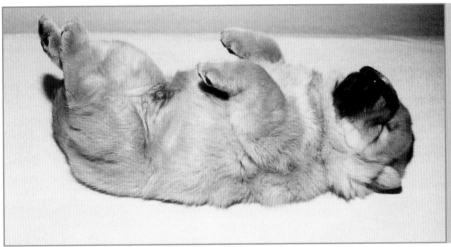

This four-week-old pup is getting used to lying on his back, as eventually he will be trained to this position for part of his grooming routine. This is also beneficial for teaching the dog to be comfortable in a submissive posture.

puppy and talk to him. Petting the puppy makes the puppy feel loved and a part of the pack. If you don't have a young son or daughter, or a niece or nephew, enlist the help of some friendly neighborhood kids. You must let your puppy meet little people. Encourage the pup to play into your home, pick up your puppy and hand him to the newcomer so that the puppy will become used to being handled by more than one individual. Have the neighborhood children visit your puppy and show them how to hold the puppy in their laps and pet him, under your

Chapter 7

Pictured at ten weeks old, Mimi is off to a great start, getting lots of love, petting and attention.

supervision, of course! When he has had his vaccinations, take him on short trips in the car with you so that he will become accustomed to riding in a car.

Since Chows can feel threatened by strangers, it is important that you let

If the puppy is destined for the show ring, then you are wise to begin opening his mouth several times a day. Do it gently and make it fun. If the puppy thinks it's a game, he'll be more amenable. You also want to handle your male puppy's testicles so that

While neither of this pair is grinning from ear to ear, at least they tolerate each other enough to sit still for a photo.

strangers pet him when you are out and about with your puppy. Ask the individual who is interested in your puppy to bend over to his level and pet him. And then, when he is ready and old enough, take him to a local dog show so that he can become used to other dogs and a crowd of people.

he gets accustomed to this type of inspection. The dog-show judge must check the Chow's teeth and testicles in the ring. It's no fun for a handler to stand over his uncooperative Chow while the dog-show judge gingerly tries to pry open the dog's jaws. Happy, playful puppies make the best show dogs.

Once you have trained your Chow puppy to stand still and to gait on a lead, as well as to have his teeth and testicles touched, you can enter your puppy in a match show. You should be calm and confident, and your Chow will take your cue. Dog shows are excellent places for socialization, meeting other dogs and people who are receptive to all kinds of canines.

Another fun part of socializing the Chow is taking him out! You want to bring your Chow everywhere possible: the mall, the park, the boardwalk, the lake, the family reunion. Anywhere dogs are allowed to go! Maybe you can bring your pup to show-and-tell at your children's school. The more unfamiliar environments to which you can introduce your Chow puppy, the better. If you have a dog park in your neighborhood, this is an excellent way to socialize the puppy with other dogs. Some

The pup's earliest socialization and life lessons come from his mom and litter-mates, invaluable education about how to be a dog!

puppies are aggressive toward other dogs, so this will require a little interaction and encouragement. Do not pull on your Chow's leash while he's meeting another dog. Dog fights most often occur when two nervous owners are yanking on their dogs' leads instead of just allowing the dogs to sniff and posture and get to know each other.

Socializing doesn't happen overnight. Your Chow needs to be included in your activities daily. If you neglect to include your Chow in outings or family gatherings, he may regress. You must be responsible for the total socialization of your Chow. This is the only way to have a reliable, friendly, personable Chow Chow who is a pleasure to own and present.

SOCIALIZING THE CHOW CHOW PUPPY

Overview

- The importance of socializing a Chow Chow from an early age cannot be overemphasized.
- Chow breeders should only breed from dogs with friendly, sound temperaments.
- A Chow must be handled and loved as a puppy or else he will not be easy to approach as an adult.
- Socializing your puppy includes handling him, petting him, accustoming him to having his mouth and feet touched, introducing him to all family members, acquainting him with strangers, allowing him to meet and play with other dogs, taking him to different places in the car. . .the list goes on!
- Socialization is an ongoing process, starting from puppyhood, in which you try to make your Chow as well rounded, well adjusted and open to new things as possible.

CHAPTER 8

House-training Your Chow Chow

Your dog must be housebroken, and this job should begin as soon as you bring him home. Diligence during the first two or three weeks will surely pay off, and this should be a relatively easy job, since the Chow is said to be an extremely easy dog to housebreak, often being trained within a week.

Every time your puppy wakes up from a nap, he should be quickly taken outside. Watch him and praise him with "Good boy!" when he urinates or defecates. Give him a pat

In order to live with any dog, the dog must have clean toileting habits. Teaching your Chow pup to relieve himself outdoors is the key to a harmonious relationship.

on the head and take him back inside. He may have a few accidents but, with the appropriate "No" from you, he will quickly learn that it is better to go outside and do his "job" than to do it on the kitchen floor and be scolded.

You will soon learn the habits of your dog. However, at the following times it is essential to take your dog out: when he gets up in the morning, after he eats, before he goes to bed and after long naps. As adults, most dogs will only have to go out three or four times a day. Some dogs will go to the door and bark when they want to be let out and others will nervously circle around. Watch and learn from your puppy's signs. Of course, crates are a major help in housebreaking, as most dogs will not want to dirty their living quarters.

Introduce your pup to his crate as soon as he comes home so he learns that this is his new "house." This is

Your Chow must be accustomed to his leash for outdoor potty trips and all other training. Eventually your Chow won't even notice that the leash is there.

Starrlett is cozy in her crate, her own special den. The key to training is teaching the dog that his crate is a happy place, one in which he can rest and relax, and one that he wants to keep clean.

best accomplished with dog treats. For the first day or two, toss a tiny treat into the crate to entice him to go in. Pick a crate command, such as "Kennel," "Inside" or "Crate," and use it every time he enters. You also can feed his first few meals inside the crate with the door still open so that the crate association will be a happy one.

Your puppy should sleep in his crate from his very first night. He may whine at first and object to the confinement. Be strong and stay the course. If you release him when he cries, you provide his first life lesson...if I cry, I get out and maybe hugged. A better scheme is to place the crate next to your bed at night for the first few weeks. Your presence will comfort him, and you'll also know if he needs a midnight potty trip. Whatever you do, do not lend comfort by taking the puppy into bed with you. To a dog, on the bed means equal, which is not a

good idea this early on when you are trying to establish your leadership role.

Make a practice of placing your puppy into his crate for naps, at nighttime and whenever you are unable to watch him closely. Not to worry...he will let you know when he wakes up and needs a potty trip. If he falls asleep under the table and wakes up when you're not there, guess what he'll do first? Make a puddle, then toddle over to say "Hi!"

Become a Chow vigilante. Routines, consistency and an eagle eye are your keys to house-training success. Puppies always "go" when they wake up (quickly now!), within a few minutes after eating, after play periods and after brief periods of confinement. Most pups under 12 weeks of age will need to eliminate at least every hour or so, which can mean ten or more times a day! (Set your oven timer to remind you.)

Always take the puppy outside to the same area, telling him "Outside" as you go out. Pick a "potty" term ("Hurry up," "Go potty" and "Get busy" are the most commonly used) and use it area so he can find it when he needs it. Watch for sniffing and circling or other signs that signal he has to relieve himself. Don't allow him to roam the house until he's house-trained; how will he find that outside

A big part of house-training is control, determining to which rooms your dog will and will not be granted access. Gidget and Dreamer are kept safely confined in their designated area by a gate barricading the hallway.

when he does his business, lavishing him with "Good puppy!" praise and repeating your key word. Use the same exit door for these potty trips, and confine puppy to the exit door if he's three or four rooms away? He does not have a house map in his head.

Of course, he will have accidents. All puppies do. If you catch him in the act, clap your hands loudly, say "Aaah! Aaah!" and scoop him up to go outside. Your voice should startle him and make him stop. Be sure to praise when he finishes his duty outside.

If you discover the piddle spot after the fact…more than three or four seconds later…you're too late. Pups only understand in the moment, and will not understand a correction given more than five seconds (that's only *five*) after the deed. Correcting any later will only cause fear and confusion. Just forget it and vow to be more vigilant.

It won't take long for a pup to find his favorite relief spot! Trees are always popular with dogs.

Despite its many benefits, crate use can be abused. Puppies under 12 weeks of age should never be confined for more than two hours at a time, unless, of course, they are sleeping. A general rule of thumb is three hours maximum for a three-month-old pup, four to five hours for the four- to five-month-old, and no more than six hours for dogs over six months of age. If you're unable to be home to release the dog, arrange for a relative, neighbor or dogsitter to let him out to exercise and potty.

Punishment has *no* place in potty training. Never rub your puppy's nose in his mistake or strike your puppy or adult dog with your hand, a newspaper or other object to correct him. He will not understand and will only become fearful of the person who is hitting him. Likewise, do not use the crate for punishment. Successful crate use depends on your puppy's positive association with his "home-within-a-home." If the crate represents punishment or "bad dog stuff," he will resist using it as his safe place. Sure, you can crate your pup after he has sorted through the trash to keep him from being underfoot as you clean up. Just don't do it in an angry fashion or tell him "Bad dog, crate!"

Most importantly, remember that successful house-training revolves around consistency and repetition.

Maintain a strict schedule and use your key words consistently. Well-trained owners have well-trained pups...and clean, nice-smelling houses!

Once he knows the routine, toileting will be exactly that: routine! This Chow has done his business and is waiting to come back inside.

HOUSE-TRAINING YOUR CHOW CHOW

Overview

- The first training you will do with your Chow pup is house-training, teaching him proper toileting habits.
- The crate is a huge help in house-training when used properly. It helps the pup learn to "hold it" and reinforces his innate desire to keep his living quarters clean.
- Take the pup out often to avoid accidents in the house. Learn to recognize the signals that mean he has to go out. Many accidents are the owner's fault, not the pup's!
- Praise your pup as he's doing his duty in the right place. Only scold him for accidents if you actually catch him in the act.
- Use the crate correctly, lots of praise, an eagle eye and a consistent schedule, and your intelligent Chow should not take long to housebreak.

Teaching Basic Commands

Chow Chow puppies are more intelligent than most breeds of dog though not necessarily easier to train. Look at the intensity and intelligence in the face of this ten week old.

Your puppy should have a good head start with socialization when you bring him home. He will be used to family and visitors, and average noises in the house and outdoors will not startle him. Socialization for your puppy is very important, and good breeders will begin with their pups before they go to new homes.

As we've discussed, let your Chow meet the neighbors and let him play a few minutes. Take him for short walks in public places where he will see people and other dogs as well as hear strange noises. Watch other dogs, however, as you do not know how your Chow or the other dogs will react. When meeting people, keep your dog on a short leash and you will have control over him so he does not jump up on anyone.

It is absolutely necessary to have a mannerly dog; therefore, there are some basic commands that you and your Chow must understand to make your dog a better citizen. One of the family members should attend puppy kindergarten classes, from which all further training will grow. This is a class that accepts puppies from two to five months of age and takes about two months to complete. You will cover the basics, like sit, heel, down and recall (or come). There are definite advantages to each. Sit and heel are great helps when walking your dog. Who needs a puppy walking between your legs, lunging

With more than one dog, the patience and dedication to training required by the owner is multiplied!

Holding your Chow pup's interest during training is essential if you are to make any progress. Chows bore easily, and you don't want this to be your pup's reaction to your instruction.

forward or lagging behind, in general acting like a nut? Have your dog walking like a gentleman on your left side and sitting as you wait to cross the street. Recall is very important for your Chow's safety if he escapes from the yard, breaks his leash or otherwise gets away from you and you need to call him back. Remember, it is essential to have an obedient Chow for both good manners and safety.

Here is a short rundown of the commands. If you attend puppy classes or obedience training classes, you will have professional help in learning these commands. However, you and your dog can learn these very basic exercises on your own.

THE PUPPY'S NAME

One of the important factors in training a young pup is to give him a name. Sometimes it may take a week or so before you find a name that fits the dog. Other times, you will have the puppy named before you bring him home. In general, short, one-syllable names are the easiest for training, such as "Stay, Lang." It becomes more difficult when you have to say, "Down, Ting-A-Ling" or "Sit, Yang Tzu Fu." You want a name that not only fits the personality of the dog but one that fits the breed itself. Rather than naming your Chow Spot, Tiny or anything too common or Western, you might want to call him something appro- priate to his heritage. Try a good Chinese name like Ming or Tang and your dog will quickly know that you are talking about him!

SIT COMMAND

This is the first exercise that you should attempt. Place your dog on your left side as you are standing and say "Sit" firmly. As you say this, run your hand down your dog's back and gently push him into a sitting position. Praise him, hold him in this position for a few minutes, release your hand, praise him again and give him a treat. Repeat this several times a day, perhaps as many as ten times. Before long, your pup will understand what you want when you say "Sit."

STAY COMMAND

Teach your dog to stay in a seated position until you call him. Have your dog sit and, as you say "Stay," place your hand in front of his nose and take a step or two, no more at the beginning, away. After ten seconds or so, call your dog. If he gets up before the end of the command, have him sit again and repeat the stay command. When he stays until called (remembering to start

When beginning to teach the sit, demonstrate the correct position by gently guiding your Chow into it the first few times.

with a very short period of time), praise him and give him a treat. As he learns this command, increase the space that you move away from the dog as well as the length of time that he stays.

HEEL COMMAND

Have your dog on your left side, with his leash on, and teach him to walk with you. If your pup lunges forward, give the leash a quick snap and say a firm "No." Then continue to walk your dog, praising him as he walks nicely by your side. Again, if he lunges, snap his leash quickly and say a smart "No." He will quickly learn that it is easier and more pleasant to walk by your side. Never allow him to lunge at someone passing by you.

COME COMMAND

This command has life-saving potential...preventing your Chow from running into the street, chasing a squirrel, following a child on a bike...the list goes on and on.

Always practice this command on leash. You can't afford to risk failure, or your pup will learn that he does not have to come when called. Once you have the pup's attention, call him from a short distance with "Puppy, Come!" (use your happy voice!) and give a treat when he comes to you. If he hesitates, tug him to you gently with his leash. Grasp and hold his collar with one hand as you dispense the treat. This is important. You will eventually phase out the treat and switch to hands-on praise. This maneuver also connects holding his collar with coming and treating, which will assist you in countless future behaviors. Do 10 or 12 repetitions 2 or 3 times a day. Once pup has mastered the come command, continue to practice daily to imprint this most important behavior onto his brain. Experienced Chow owners know, however, that you can never completely trust a dog to come when called if the dog is bent on a self-appointed mission. "Off leash" is often synonymous with "out of control," so it is always wise to keep your Chow on lead unless in a securely enclosed area.

DOWN COMMAND

This will probably be the most difficult of the basic commands to teach, as some dogs resist the down position. Place your dog in the sit position and kneel down next to him. Place your right hand under his front legs and your left hand on his shoulders. As you say "Down," gently push his front legs out into the down position. Once you have him down, talk gently to him, stroke his back so that he will be comfortable and then praise him.

OTHER HELPFUL COMMANDS

There are some commands that are not taught in obedience class that you and your dog will learn on your own. "Off" is an important command, as a Chow will become tall enough to finish off the candy dish on the coffee table or reach on the kitchen table for the butter. "Off, Tang" and then push him down on his four feet. Again, dogs are smart, particularly Chows, and he will quickly

Once your Chow is reliable with the sit, which should not take long, you can move on to teaching him to stay in the sit position.

learn what "Off" means.

Another good command is "Kennel up" to tell the dog to go to his crate. Along with "Kennel up" you will teach

hours. And, of course, the most basic of commands, which is learned very quickly, is "No." Say it firmly and with conviction. Again, your dog

Unless your Chow Chow is a flawless, perfectly trained show dog, don't encourage him to jump up on you.

"Bedtime!" which also means to go to his crate. Do not confuse the two! Dogs quickly learn that "Bedtime" means a treat and to bed for the night, while "Kennel up" means that you will be back in a few

will learn that this means to keep off, don't do it or don't even think about it.

A FEW MORE TIPS

In all of your commands, you must be fair (don't tell him to sit when he is already sitting), you must be consistent (don't let him jump onto the sofa sometimes and not at other times) and you must be firm in speaking all commands. After the dog does what you want, give him a pat on the head and praise, "Good dog, Mai." If he has achieved some great success, give him a treat along with the praise.

Big parts of training are patience, persistence and routine. Teach each command the same way every time, do not lose your patience with the dog, as he will not understand what you are doing, and reward him for performing his command properly. With a Chow, you will find that your puppy will learn these commands very quickly. Your friends, when they come to your house for a dinner party, will also appreciate a well-behaved dog who will not jump on their clothing or land in their laps while they are having cocktails.

TEACHING BASIC COMMANDS

Overview

- Your pup's knowledge of the basic commands serves as the foundation for his overall good behavior.
- Teaching commands to your pup is essential not only for his good manners but also for his safety.
- Choose a fitting name for your Chow puppy and use it often so that he learns to recognize it.
- The basic commands include sit, stay, come, down and heel. In addition, "Off" and "No," as well as commands that tell him to go to his crate, will be very helpful.
- Use lots of encouragement and praise, and of course treats now and then, to motivate and reward your Chow during his lessons.

CHAPTER 10

Home Care for Your Chow Chow

Your Chow's health is in your hands between his annual visits to the vet. Be ever conscious of any changes in his appearance or behavior. Things to consider:

Has your Chow gained a few too many pounds or suddenly lost weight? Are his teeth clean and white or does he need some plaque attackers? Is he urinating more frequently, drinking more water than usual? Does he strain during a bowel movement? Any changes in his appetite? Does he appear short of

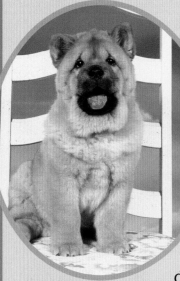

Caring for your Chow Chow is an everyday responsibility. Keep your dog sitting pretty throughout his life with a home-care routine that focuses on wellness and keeping him in top condition.

breath, lethargic, overly tired? Have you noticed limping or any sign of joint stiffness?

These are all signs of serious health problems that you should discuss with your vet as soon as they appear. This is especially important for the senior dog, since even minor changes can be a sign of something serious.

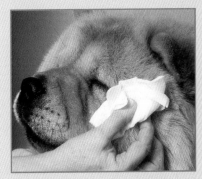

Keep your Chow's eyes and the areas around them clean; also have ointment on hand in case of an eye injury.

FIRST AID

Every home with a pet should have a first aid kit. You should acquire all of the necessary items to have on hand, kept together in a box or kit to have handy when you need them. Here are some basic items that you will need:

- Alcohol for cleaning a wound;
- Antibiotic salve for treating the wound;
- Over-the-counter eye wash in case your dog gets something in his eyes or just needs to have his eyes cleaned—"to get the red out";

Bee stings, insect bites, pollen allergies and heat exhaustion are among the hazards a dog may encounter while enjoying the great outdoors. Have a well-stocked canine first aid kit and familiarize yourself with the signs of problems.

- Forceps for pulling out wood ticks, thorns and burs;
- Styptic powder for when a toenail has been trimmed too short and bleeds;
- Rectal thermometer;
- A nylon stocking to be used as a muzzle if your pet should be badly injured.

Most of these items can be purchased very reasonably from your local drug store. For everyday common-sense care, every dog owner should know the signs of an emergency. Many dog agencies, humane societies and animal shelters sponsor canine first aid seminars. Participants learn how to recognize and deal with signs of common emergency situations, how to assemble a first aid kit, how to give CPR to a dog and more. The moral here is…know your Chow. Early detection is the key to your dog's quality of life.

STAYING WELL

Once your dog is mature and remaining well, he will only need a yearly visit to the veterinary clinic for a check-up and booster shots for his vaccines. At these visits, you may want to have the veterinarian check his teeth and express his anal glands.

You may purchase a dental tool and clean the teeth yourself. Set the dog on the grooming table, with his head in the noose, and gently scrape away any tartar. Some animals will let you do this and others will not. A hard dog biscuit every night before bedtime will help to keep the tartar down as well as regular toothbrushing, and you can save the dental scraping for the vet.

Expressing the anal glands is not the greatest of tasks, besides being quite smelly, and you may find that it is easier to have this done during the yearly trip to the clinic. On occasion, the anal glands will become impacted, requiring veterinary assistance to clean out.

By now, you know your

dog well, you know how much he eat and sleeps and how hard he plays. As with all of us, on occasion he may "go off his feed" or appear to be sick. If he has been nauseated for 24 to 36 hours, or had diarrhea for the same amount of time or has drunk excessive water for five or six days, a trip to the veterinarian is in order. Make your appointment and tell the receptionist why you need the appointment right away. The veterinarian will ask you the following questions:

• When did your dog last eat a normal meal?

• How long has he had diarrhea or been vomiting?

• Has he eaten anything in the last 24 hours?

• Could he have eaten a toy or a piece of clothing or anything else unusual?

• Is he drinking more water than usual?

The veterinarian will check him over, take his temperature and pulse, listen to his heart, feel his stomach for any lumps,

look at his gums and teeth for color and check his eyes and ears. He will probably also draw blood to run tests.

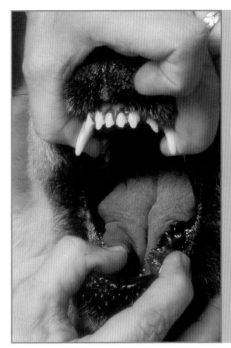

Home dental care is a huge part of your dog's maintenance program. Get in the habit of brushing his teeth at least once weekly and regularly checking the overall health of his mouth and gums.

At the end of the examination, the vet will make his diagnosis and suggest how best to treat the problem. He may send your dog home with you with some antibiotics, take some x-rays, keep the dog overnight for observation or recommend another course of treatment. Follow your veterinarian's instructions and you will find that very often your dog will be back to normal in a day or two. In the meantime, feed him light meals and keep him quiet, perhaps confined to his crate.

Parasites can be a problem and there are certain ones of which you should be aware. Heartworm can be a deadly problem, and some parts of the country can be more prone to this than others. Heartworms become very massive and wrap themselves around the dog's heart. If not treated, the dog will eventually die. In the spring, call your veterinarian and ask if your dog should have a heartworm test. If so, take him to the clinic and he will be given a test to make certain that he is clear of heartworm; he then will be put on heartworm preventative medication. This is important, particularly if you live in areas where mosquitoes are present.

Fleas are also a problem but particularly in the warmer parts of the country. You can purchase flea powder or a flea collar from the pet shop or ask your veterinarian what he suggests that you use. Today there are many effective spot-on treatments available from the vet. If you suspect fleas, lay your dog on his side, separate the coat to the skin and see if you see any skipping, jumping or skittering around of little bugs.

Ticks are more prevalent in grassy and wooded areas. Ticks are small (to start) and dark, and they like to attach themselves to the warm parts of the ears, the leg pits, face folds, etc. The longer they are on the dog, the bigger they become, filling themselves with your pet's blood and becoming as big as a dime. Take your forceps and carefully pull the tick out to make sure you get the pincers. Promptly flush the tick down the toilet or light a match to it. Put rubbing alcohol on the wound and a dab of antibiotic salve.

Let common sense and a

would say is "Who are you calling a Chow-hound?" No Chow has ever been accused of having a poor appetite! To determine if your Chow is

The nose knows when it's time for dinner! A good-quality diet, providing balanced and complete nutrition, is essential for any dog and will be reflected in overall health, coat condition, temperament and activity level.

good veterinarian be your guide in coping with these and other health issues.

WEIGHT CONTROL

If your Chow could suddenly speak, the first thing that he

overweight, you should be able to feel your dog's ribs beneath a thin layer of muscle with very gentle pressure on his rib cage. When viewing your dog from above, you should be able to see a definite waistline; from the side, he should have an obvious tuck-up in his abdomen.

Keep a record of his weight from each annual vet visit. A few extra pounds? Adjust his

Excessive weight is especially hard on older dogs with creaky joints. A senior Chow who is sedentary will grow out of shape more quickly. Walking and running (slower for old

Keep your Chow Chow fit and trim. Don't let a glorious rough coat mask extra pounds on your Chow.

food portions (cut down on those treats), perhaps switch to a "light," "senior" or lower-calorie dog-food formula and increase his exercise.

guys) are still the best workouts for health mainte-nance. Tailor your dog's exercise to fit his age and physical condition.

ORAL HYGIENE

Now that your dog is slim and trim, let's examine his teeth. The American Veterinary Dental Society states that 80% of dogs show signs of oral disease as early as age three. Further studies prove that good oral hygiene can add three to five years to a dog's life.

Danger signs include build-up of yellow and brown tartar along the gumline, red, inflamed gums and persistent bad breath. If neglected, these conditions will allow bacteria to accumulate in your dog's mouth and enter your dog's bloodstream through those damaged gums, increasing the risk for disease in the vital organs such as the heart, liver and kidneys. It's known that periodontal disease is a major contributor to kidney disease, which is a common cause of death in older dogs...and highly preventable.

Your vet should examine your Chow's teeth and gums during his annual check-ups to make sure that they are clean and healthy. The veterinarian may recommend professional cleaning if there is excessive plaque build-up.

During the other 364 days a year, you are your dog's dentist. Brush his teeth daily, or at least twice a week. Use a doggie toothbrush (designed for the contour of a canine's mouth) and use dog toothpaste flavored with chicken, beef or liver. (Minty people paste is harmful to dogs.) If your dog resists a toothbrush, try a nappy washcloth or gauze pad wrapped around your finger. Start the brushing process with gentle gum massages when your Chow is very young so he will learn to tolerate and even enjoy the process.

Feeding dry dog food is an excellent way to help minimize plaque accumulation. You can also treat your dog to a raw carrot every day. Carrots help scrub away plaque while providing extra vitamins A and C. Invest in healthy chew objects, such as nylon or rubber bones and toys with ridges that act as tartar scrapers. Certain products available at pet shops are designed to help remove and prevent plaque. Raw beef knuckle bones also work, but watch for sharp edges and splintering on these or any other chew object, which can cut the dog's mouth and intestinal lining. Rawhides do not digest easily and can cause choking if the dog swallows large chunks, as many dogs tend to do. If you offer rawhides, do so infrequently and only under supervision.

PREVENTATIVE CONCERNS

In addition to health problems, there is the usual "housekeeping" with your new puppy. When your dog is a young pup, you should start getting him used to an examination routine. Each time he is groomed, you should check over his ears, eyes and teeth.

Ears should be checked for dirt or any sign of infection. Take a damp cloth (a soft old washcloth can work quite well) and gently wipe the inside of the ear. You can use plain water or a canine ear-cleaning product available at pet-supply shops or from your veterinarian.

If you notice any build-up of wax, or a putrid smell, you should take your Chow to the veterinarian to have his ears looked at. If there is an infection, the vet will prescribe an ointment or liquid to clear up the problem. Dogs with upright ears have more of a chance of getting dirt into the ears, whereas dogs with drop ears have "warm" ears where infections can grow more easily. If you see your dog shaking his head from side to side, or pushing his head and ear along the side of the furniture, you can be almost certain that an ear infection is in the making.

Another problem to watch out for is ear-mite infestation. This is usually recognized by dark-brown droppings in the ear and the dog's shaking his head, pawing at his ears and/or scratching his ears. In this case, your vet will prescribe medication to eradicate the mites, usually in the form of a liquid to be administered to the dog's ears by you at home.

When grooming, take your damp washcloth and gently wash the eye area. Dogs with folds around the eyes and nostrils like your Chow can have a build-up of matter that should be cleaned out daily.

All dogs should have their eyes checked if any redness appears. Quite often you can purchase an over-the-counter medication at the pet shop to clear up the redness. If an eye problem persists or if you notice other abnormalities such as cloudiness in the eye,

mucus from the eye or excessive tearing, you will have to see your veterinarian.

We've discussed that teeth should also be brushed on a regular basis, and this is

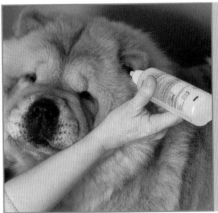

Keep your Chow's ears clean with soft wipes, never probing inside the ear canal. There may be times when your vet prescribes a medicated cleansing solution.

something to which you should accustom your puppy at an early age, perhaps as part of his grooming routine. It will be very difficult to begin brushing an adult Chow's teeth, as he likely will resist this type of handling if he is not used to it. If you allow plaque to build up, your dog will have as many dental problems as you would have. Veterinarians will clean your dog's teeth, but it is a costly process and does not need to be done by a professional if you have done your work at home. Giving your dog several dog biscuits a day, plus his dry kibble, will help prevent the build-up of plaque.

As a dog ages, as in humans, his gums may recede and he may encounter further dental problems along with unpleasant-smelling

Slobber happens! Have a cloth handy for wiping around your Chow's mouth, especially following meals or water breaks.

breath. Your vet may tell you that it is necessary to remove one or more teeth, but most dogs will continue to eat well even if all of their teeth have been pulled. Of course, their

diet will be a bit different, but they will fare just as well. A distinct unpleasant odor from the mouth is a signal that all is not well with your dog's gums or teeth.

When going over your Chow's coat with a brush, you want to both look and feel for lumps, bumps and parasites. Likewise, hot spots, a form of dermatitis that is self-inflicted by the dog, are common problems in heavily coated dogs like the Chow. These hot spots can form around the dog's rear region, under his tail or on a limb. The dog itches and bites at a spot so severely that he creates an open wound. Veterinarians can treat these with topical solutions and maybe antibiotics, depending on the cause of the itching, although the causes of hot spots cannot always be determined.

All dogs have anal sacs located on either side of the rectum. The contents, very smelly, are used to mark the dog's territory and are usually released when the dog defecates. Occasionally these glands will have to be expressed by hand. Have your veterinarian show you how to do this the first time and then you can do it at home, even though it is a rather smelly and unpleasant job! A sign that the anal glands are clogged is when your dog scoots across the floor on his fanny. On occasion, the glands will appear swollen, which can be seen on a smooth-coated dog.

The eyes, ears, teeth, skin, coat and anal glands are part of the general housekeeping of a dog. Start your dog on this cleaning routine at a very early age, doing a bit at a time, and when your dog is an adult you will have little difficulty in performing these functions, all of which are very important for your dog's overall maintenance and preventative care.

HOME CARE FOR YOUR CHOW CHOW

Overview

- Have a well-stocked first aid kit as well as knowledge of basic canine first aid techniques.
- Be aware of changes in your Chow, including his behavior, weight, appetite, thirst and sleeping habits; sudden changes may indicate a health problem.
- Discuss a safe preventative program for internal and external parasites.
- Weight control and home dental care are two essentials of keeping your Chow in good overall condition.
- "Housekeeping" concerns include maintenance of the dog's eyes, ears and anal sacs, in addition to his skin and coat condition.

Grooming Your Chow Chow

Do understand before purchasing your Chow that he will need grooming and attention to his hygiene. The Chow, both the smooth- and rough-coated variety, will certainly require grooming; however, the rough-coated, the more common of the two varieties, will obviously require more grooming.

The following tools will be among those required: a grooming table, a wire slicker brush and a pin brush. You will also need a good pair of scissors and toenail clippers. You will likely find it convenient to have a coat conditioner

A real bathing beauty: a hooded Chow puppy right out of the bath!

and a spray bottle as well.

Begin when the puppy is very young. Lay him on his side on the grooming table and gently start at his spine, brushing the coat back toward the table, using your coat conditioner when necessary. Brush down to the skin and work out any mats that you come across. Mats can be worked out with either your comb or your fingers and then your comb. However, if you groom your Chow twice a week you will not have many mats in the coat. If you let a mat go, you will soon have a difficult problem and may have to cut the mat out, which will not contribute to the lovely-looking Chow coat that you want!

Groom the legs the same way, again with the Chow lying on his side. When you have completed one side, turn the dog over on his other side and finish your job. When your puppy is dropping his puppy coat, you will find that you will be grooming him

A gentle child can certainly help with the grooming tasks. By spending a few minutes each day brushing the pup, the child helps foster a bond with her canine "sibling," which is so important with the Chow Chow.

A metal shedding blade is a helpful tool for removing dead hair, which can be especially abundant on a Rough Chow.

CHAPTER 11

often to prevent the puppy coat from matting in with the new coat growth. If you start the brushing process when your puppy is very young, working for short periods of time so that neither he nor you lose your patience, you will find that your dog will enjoy his grooming sessions. It is important to take the time in puppyhood to teach your Chow to lie on his side so that you don't end up struggling to get an uncooperative adult into this position.

When you have finished brushing out the coat, stand your dog up on the table. With your scissors, trim around his feet to neaten

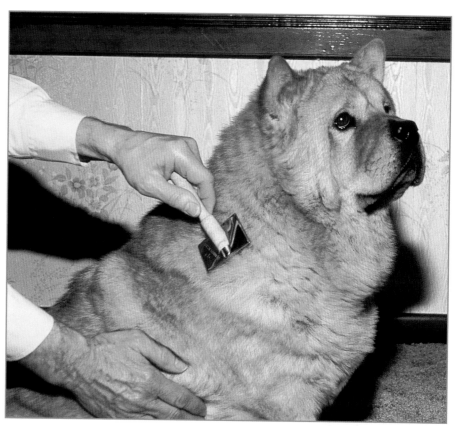

A slicker brush is used over the body of this Smooth Chow.

them up. Also check the footpads and trim any excess hair between them. You may or may not want to trim off his whiskers.

As your Chow matures, you will use the pin brush

Grooming can and should be a pleasant time for both you and your dog. Be sure not to overdo it for both of you, never working so long that your dog becomes snappy or you

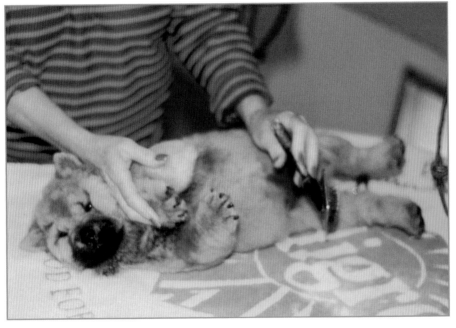

Lay your puppy on his side to brush him. Get him in the habit of cooperating from puppy-hood, before his mind is made up about what he likes and what he doesn't.

on him more than the slicker brush. And you will find that both your pin brush and slicker brush will eventually wear down. When the pins fall into the rubber backing, it is time to buy a new pin brush.

become short-tempered, making the job no longer easy or fun. Consider how much time you and your Chow will spend together in grooming over the course of his life, and you'll quickly understand why it's essential to make grooming a positive experience.

A Chow will require a bath very rarely, provided that he has been groomed with regularity. This is

It is important to trim your dog's toenails, and it is best to start this within a week of bringing him home. Purchase a quality toenail trimmer for pets. You may want to

An alfresco dip is a lot more pleasant than a soapy bath, especially on a hot day.

basically an odor-free breed, and frequent bathing will just dry out his skin and coat. If a bath is necessary, stop at your local pet store and pick up a good-quality dry-bath product.

purchase a styptic stick in case you trim a nail too short and bleeding starts. If your dog's toenails are light in color, you will easily see the blood vessel that runs inside the nail. However, it is a bit more difficult to see in dark-nailed dogs and you may nick the blood vessel until you are more familiar with trimming the nails. In this case, you will need to stem the flow of blood right away, and a styptic stick is handy to have nearby. If you do not start trimming the nails at a young age, so your dog is used to this, you will have greater difficulty in trimming the nails as the dog becomes

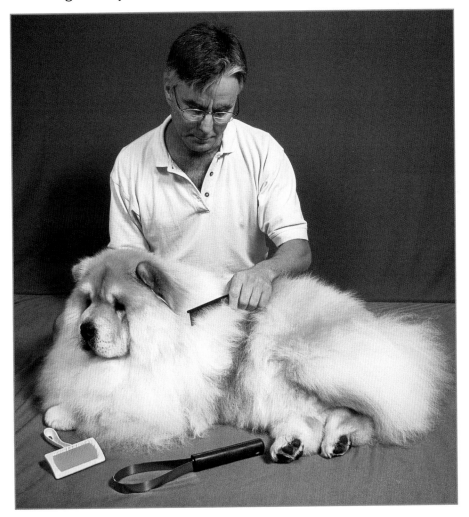

A metal comb is used gently on the Rough Chow's mane to ensure that the long, dense hair in this area stays mat- and tangle-free.

A pre-show primping on the grooming table. For heavily groomed breeds like the Chow, a grooming table is a good idea to make both of you more comfortable during grooming sessions.

larger, heavier and more difficult to hold.

The best way to trim a Chow Chow's toenails is with an electric grinder with a sandpaper head. Most Chows hate having their feet touched, no matter how young you start the process. The grinder makes this chore somewhat easier. To introduce the puppy to the grinder, you should first accustom him to the sound of the motor. Place the grinder on a table and turn it on. Let the puppy hear the noise while you're playing with him. Once you notice that the noise isn't upsetting the puppy, you can try to grind one nail (maybe two, provided the first nail goes well). Another advantage to the grinder is that you never have to worry about nicking the blood vessel, the grinder will instantly cauterize the quick should you nick it.

GROOMING YOUR CHOW CHOW

Overview

- While the Rough Chow will need more grooming, both varieties are abundantly coated and require an owner's attention.
- Begin brushing your puppy with gentle strokes to accustom him to the procedure.
- It is easiest to train your Chow to lie on his side on a grooming table for part of his grooming, allowing you to attend to all of the hard-to-reach areas.
- Frequent brushing will prevent matting. If mats form, they will be difficult to remove, making grooming unpleasant for you and your Chow.
- Frequent bathing is neither necessary nor recommended.
- Check your Chow's nails at each grooming session, grinding or clipping them as needed.

CHAPTER 12

Keeping Your Chow Chow Active

M any owners and their dogs are looking for something challenging, and there are many activities to keep both of you very busy, active and interested. Chows can excel in many activities because of their intelligence, their willingness to please and their tenacity. After puppy kindergarten, you may want to work toward a Canine Good Citizen® Award. This program, when success-

Conformation showing is popular among all breeds, and the Chow's regal presence in the ring is a sure attention-getter.

fully completed, shows that your dog will mind his manners at home, in public places and with other dogs. This class is available to all dogs of all ages. It's a fun course and useful for everyday life, especially in a breed like the Chow in which socialization is so important.

Although not traditionally thought of as a top obedience trial contender, the Chow is capable of success in this sport with much dedication to his training.

There are ten steps, including accepting a friendly stranger, sitting politely for petting, accepting light grooming and examination from a stranger, walking on a loose lead, coming when called, responding calmly to another dog, responding to distractions, down on command and remaining calm when the owner is out of sight for three minutes. Upon successful completion, your Chow will receive an AKC Canine Good Citizen® certificate.

Obedience is a long-established sport that Chows can enjoy. Obedience trials are held either by themselves or in conjunction with a conformation

Multi-Ch. Mimi poses on the agility dog walk, representing one of the areas of canine competition in which she's enjoyed success.

show. The first level is Novice, whereupon completion of three passing "legs," the dog will earn a Companion Dog (CD) title. Open is the second level, and the dog earns a Companion Dog Excellent (CDX) title upon completion of three successful legs. The next class is Utility (UD), which includes off-lead work, silent hand signals and picking the right dumbbells from a group of dumbbells. Not many dogs reach this level, and it is a major accomplishment for both owner and dog when a Utility Dog degree is achieved.

Agility, started in England, is a relatively new sport in the US and can be easily found at dog shows. Look for the large, noisy ring filled with competitors and dogs running around the obstacle course, with excited spectators watching at ringside, joining in with cheers.

Dogs are taught to run a course that includes hurdles, ladders, jumps and a variety of other challenges. There are a number of titles in agility, depending upon the obstacles that the dog is able to conquer as well as his speed and accuracy. AKC defines agility as, "The enjoyment of bringing together communication, training, timing, accuracy and just plain fun in the ultimate game for you and your dog." Lots of exercise for both dog and owner, and your Chow may or may not enjoy this type of activity.

The ultimate in degrees is the Versatile Companion Dog. This is the degree that recognizes those dogs and handlers who have been successful in multiple dog sports. In order to excel at any of these activities, it is essential to belong to a club or training class where there is equipment and facilities for practice. Find a good school in your area and attend a class as a spectator before enrolling. If you like the facility, the instructor and the type of instruction, sign your dog up for the next series of lessons.

Canine sports have become so popular with the public that there should be little difficulty in finding a training facility. You will find it a great experience to work with your dog and meet new people with whom you will have a common interest. This will all take time and interest on your part, and a willing dog working on the other end of the leash.

Of course, the easiest way to keep your dog active and fit is to take him for a walk every morning and evening. This will be good for you, too! Playing games with your dog will delight him and strengthen your bond. Make sure that all toys are safe, sturdy and of the appropriate size, unable to be swallowed or easily destroyed.

KEEPING YOUR CHOW CHOW ACTIVE

Overview

- Keeping a dog active keeps him fit, both physically and mentally.
- Consider training your Chow for the Canine Good Citizen® test, proving that your Chow is well socialized and well adjusted, thus promoting a good image of the breed.
- Although not typically thought of as athletes, Chows certainly can be trained to compete in obedience and agility.
- Involvement in a breed club will help you find out about activities to do with your Chow.
- Daily walks provide exercise, continued socialization and time for the two of you to nurture your bond.

CHAPTER 13

Your Chow Chow and His Vet

B efore bringing your Chow home, you must find a good vet. Your breeder, if from your area, should be able to recommend someone; otherwise, it will be your job to find a clinic that you like. Considerations for finding a veterinarian are to find someone, for convenience, who is within ten miles of your home. Find a vet that you like and trust, who knows what he is doing and who has knowledge of the Chow and breed-specific issues.

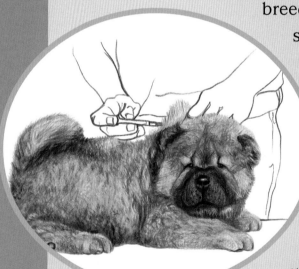

One of the first things you and your new Chow puppy will do together is visit the vet, where the pup will get a thorough health check and the vet will set up a schedule for the pup's vaccinations.

See that the office looks and smells clean. It is your right to check on fees before setting up an appointment, and you will usually need an appointment. If you have a satisfactory visit, take the business card so that you have the clinic's number and the name of the veterinarian that you saw. Try and see the same vet at each visit, as he will personally know the history of your dog and your dog will be familiar with him.

Keep your medical-supply kit stocked and ready with items for routine use as well as those for emergency care should the need for first aid arise.

Inquire whether the clinic takes emergency calls and, if they do not, as many no longer do, get the name, address and telephone number of the emergency veterinary service in your area. Keep this number handy with your vet's phone number.

On your first visit, take along the documentation from your breeder detailing the shots that your puppy has had, so that the vet will know which series of shots your pup

What's itching your Chow? It may be nothing out of the ordinary, but the Chow's abundant coat can hide lumps, bumps, rashes, parasites and other problems.

should be getting. You should also take in a fecal sample for a worm test.

The recommended vaccines are for distemper, infectious canine hepatitis, parvovirus infections and parainfluenza. Although this seems like an impressive list of shots, there is one shot that will cover all of the major viruses...DHLPP. This series of shots will start between six and ten weeks, which means that the breeder will be giving the first shots to the litter and the vet will have to finish up the series of three shots, given at four-week intervals.

Distemper at one time was the scourge of dog breeding, but with the proper immunization and a clean puppy-rearing area, this no longer presents a problem to the reputable breeder. Canine hepatitis, very rare in the United States, is a severe liver infection caused by a virus. Leptospirosis is an uncommon disease that affects the kidneys;

it is rare in young puppies, occurring primarily in adult dogs. Parvovirus is recognized by fever, vomiting and diarrhea. This is a deadly disease for pups and can spread very easily through their feces. The vaccine is highly effective in prevention.

SPECIFIC HEALTH CONCERNS

Chows, like other dogs, do have some health problems specific to the breed. All Chow owners should be aware of these problems.

HYPOTHYROIDISM

A decreased functioning of the thyroid is the most common of hormonal disorders in dogs. Clinical signs will appear anywhere between two and six years of age, with the same probability of occurrence in males and females. Often the dog will show lethargy, being unable or unwilling to exercise, and a tendency to gain weight. The onset of the disease is very gradual and may not be noticed until thyroid therapy has started and the owner can see the difference in his dog's personality and activity level. Contact your veterinarian if you suspect that this could be a problem.

HIP DYSPLASIA

A major concern, as it is in most larger breeds, hip dysplasia is an inherited disease in which the head of the femur (thigh bone) fails to fit into the socket in the hip bone and there is not enough muscle mass to hold the joint together. This can be a very painful problem for the dog, causing him to limp or to move about with great difficulty. There are various therapeutic, medical and surgical treatment methods, depending on the severity of the condition.

All Chow Chows that are bred should have normal hips as determined by an x-ray and approved by the Orthopedic Foundation for Animals (OFA). Chow Chows also have an incidence of elbow dysplasia, which is another hereditary disease. Again, x-rays should be taken of all dogs that are to be bred. If normal, these results will be registered by the OFA; only dogs cleared by the OFA, and thus assigned OFA numbers, should be used for breeding.

ENTROPION

This can be a problem in the Chow. This is an inherited condition in which the eyelashes turn inward toward the eyes and will be a cause of constant irritation. If you find that your Chow tears excessively, consult your vet for treatment.

HEAT STROKE

Heat prostration, or heat stroke, is a condition of which Chow owners should be aware because of the breed's heavy coat, whether rough or smooth. You should not take your Chow out for a walk on an excessively warm or humid day. Think of it as putting your child in a fur coat when it is a 95°F day and

CHAPTER 13

then taking her outside! If your Chow becomes overheated, it is essential to wet him down with cold water (a garden hose works the best). If he continues to be in stress, contact your veterinarian immediately.

HEART DISEASE

Heart disease is common in all canines, not specific to just the Chow, yet it is one problem that

Oh, my aching head! It's doubtful that your Chow will give you this obvious a sign that he's not feeling well, but, if you know your dog, you will be able to tell when things are not quite right.

dog owners most frequently overlook. Symptoms include panting and shortness of breath, chronic coughing, especially at night or upon first waking in the morning, and changes in sleeping habits. Heart disease can be treated if

you catch it early. Knowing your dog and recognizing changes are keys to early detection.

KIDNEY DISEASE

Kidney disease also can be treated successfully with early diagnosis. Dogs seven years and older should be tested annually for kidney and liver function. If your dog drinks excessive amounts of water and urinates more frequently, or has accidents in the house, run, don't walk, to your vet. Kidney disease can be managed with special diets to reduce the workload on the kidneys.

SPAYING/NEUTERING

Should you or shouldn't you? This is almost a non-question, since spaying/neutering is the best health insurance policy you can give your Chow. Statistics prove that females spayed before their first heat cycle (estrus) have 90% less risk of several common female cancers and other serious female health problems. Males neutered before their male hormones kick in, usually before six months of age, enjoy zero to greatly reduced risk of testicular and prostate cancer and other related tumors and infections. Additionally, males will be less likely to roam, become aggressive or display those overt male behaviors that owners find difficult to handle. Your breeder may even *require* spaying/neutering if your Chow is not destined for the show ring or a breeding program.

BE AWARE!
You should be aware of these problems within the breed and ask the breeder if he has had his dogs tested. If he has, ask to see the certificates with the registries and do not just accept his word that the sire and dam of the litter have been tested for the various problems. This list may seem daunting, but responsible breeders will have had their stock tested and will be doing their best to eliminate these problems in the breed.

YOUR CHOW CHOW AND HIS VET

Overview

- Find a vet in your area whom you like and trust and who preferably has knowledge of and experience with the Chow Chow.
- You and your pup will visit the vet soon after he comes home for an overall health check and to continue with his vaccination schedule.
- Acquaint yourself with common health problems, both those to which all breeds are prone and those specific to the Chow Chow.
- Perform regular checks of your Chow's abundant coat, getting all the way to the skin, as sometimes skin and coat problems can go unnoticed.
- Discuss all aspects of spaying/neutering with your vet.

The Aging Chow Chow

As your dog starts aging, he will start to slow down. He will not play as hard or as long as he used to and he will sleep more. He will find the sunbeam in the morning hours and take a long nap. At this time, you will probably put him on a senior-formula dog food. Continue to watch his weight, as it is more important than ever not to let your senior citizen become obese. You will notice that his muzzle will become gray and you may see opacities in his eyes, signs of cataracts. These can be corrected, but blindness can become a factor as your dog ages, caused by

As your Chow ages, dietary changes may become necessary to aid digestion, prevent obesity and help with other age-related health issues.

any of various problems.

The average lifespan for a Chow is 12 years. As your Chow becomes older, he may become arthritic. Continue your walks, making them shorter, and give him a baby aspirin when he appears to be stiff. Keep up with his grooming, as both of you will like to have him looking and smelling proper. Watch for lumps and bumps and take him to the veterinarian if you notice any abnormalities. Incontinence can also become a problem with the older dog. This is frustrating for you and hard on the house, but he hasn't become unhousebroken; rather, his excretory muscle tone is fading.

Veterinary care has changed much over the last decade or two, as has medical care for humans. Your veterinarian can now do much to extend your dog's life if you want to spend the money. Unfortunately, this will extend his life, but it will not bring

An older dog will be more inclined to take it easy, needing more frequent periods of rest.

Separation anxiety can affect dogs of any age, but even dogs not previously affected can start to experience this problem as they reach their senior years.

back his youth. Your primary concern should be to help your animal live out his life comfortably, and there are medications that can be helpful for this goal. Whatever you do, try to put your dog and his well-being and comfort ahead of your emotions and do what will be best for your pet.

Always remember the many wonderful years that your pet gave to you and your family and, with that thought, it may not be long before you are looking for a new puppy

Older dogs still benefit from exercise to keep their joints and muscles in shape, but walks should be shorter and slower, letting your Chow set the pace and rest as needed.

for the household. And there you are, back at the beginning with a cute bundle of joy, ready for another ten years or more of happiness!

THE AGING CHOW CHOW

Overview

- The Chow has an average lifespan of about 12 years. Telltale signs of aging include graying around the muzzle and an overall decrease in activity level.
- Keep giving your Chow the same good care, making accommodation for his older age.
- A senior dog benefits from more frequent trips to the vet, as early detection of any problems is important.
- Remember all of the joy that your Chow has given you during his life and do all you can to help him live out his senior years as happily and comfortably as possible.